– A GIFT FOR –

Jackie

– FROM –

DIANE with love

All my love and
friendship Dane

Copyright © 2009 by Gift Books from Hallmark,
a division of Hallmark Cards, Inc.

Visit us on the Web at Hallmark.com.

Compiled and written by Woohoo Ink, LLC
Text copyright © 2009 by Woohoo Ink, LLC
(except public domain text)

Editorial Director: Todd Hafer
Art Director: Kevin Swanson
Design: The DesignWorks Group
Production Artist: Dan Horton

ISBN: 978-1-59530-201-4

BOK3096

Printed and bound in China

DEC14

gift books

A
CELEBRATION
OF YOUR
DREAMS

G O
F O R
I T !

BEGIN

GO.

"As you journey through life, choose your destination wisely, but don't hurry there. You will arrive soon enough. Wander the back roads, the forgotten paths, the unknown ways, as you keep your dreams in your heart as the light that guides you.

Seek out new voices, strange sights, and bold ideas. Such things are riches for the soul.

And if, upon your arrival, you find that your destination is not exactly what you dreamed it would be, don't be disappointed. Think of all you would have missed if not for the journey there, and know that the true worth of your travels lies not just in where you've come to be, but in *who* you became along the way."

– LINDA STATEN –

"To travel hopefully is a better
thing than to arrive."

– ROBERT LOUIS STEVENSON –

TODAY IS
A GIFT;
THAT'S WHY
IT'S CALLED
THE *PRESENT*.

"You must begin wherever you are."

"Whatever you can do or dream you can,
begin it. Boldness has beauty,
power, and magic in it."

Beginnings are wonderful things — they're free,
they're full of possibilities, and everyone gets
a new one every day. What will you do with yours?

"I only hope that we never lose sight of one thing—that it all began with a mouse."

– WALT DISNEY –

Imagine a new stack of crisp white paper.
It's just waiting for you to start writing
the pages of your story. No one
else's story will be like yours. So fill
those pages however you wish, and
sign *your* story with a flourish.

ATTITUDE

IS THE
MASTER KEY
TO LIFE'S
LITTLE LOCKS.

"It is not a successful climb
unless you enjoy the journey."

– DAN BENSON –

"Most folks are about as happy as they
make up their minds to be."

– ABRAHAM LINCOLN –

"One person with passion is better than 40 who are merely interested."

– TOM CONNELLAN –

"Whether you think you can or think you can't, you're right."

– HENRY FORD –

"The happiness of your life depends on the quality of your thoughts."

– MARCUS ANTONIUS –

It's good to know life has a lot to
offer you, but even better to
know that you have a lot to offer life!

MY SPIRIT
TAKES FLIGHT
I AM HOPEFUL
AND FREE
TO EXPRESS,
TO EXPLORE,
TO BEGIN . . .

TO BE ME.

DREAM

"You see things; and you say, 'Why?'
But I dream things that never were;
and I say, 'Why not?'"

– GEORGE BERNARD SHAW –

A SINGLE
DREAM

CAN LAUNCH
THE JOURNEY
OF A LIFETIME.

Achievement begins with belief.

YOUR SUCCESS
CAN BE ACHIEVED
IN TWO SIMPLE STEPS:

- FIND YOUR DREAM.
- CHASE YOUR DREAM.

To dream the impossible dream
is to begin to make it possible.

"It's kind of fun to do the impossible."

– WALT DISNEY –

"Imagination is more important
than knowledge."

– ALBERT EINSTEIN –

EMBRACE
YOUR
DREAMS
WITH
PASSION!

"Act as if it were impossible to fail."

– DOROTHEA BRANDE –

"Nothing great was ever achieved
without enthusiasm."

– RALPH WALDO EMERSON –

A dream come true is just a tough little wish

that would not take **NO** for an answer.

"The man who has no imagination
has no wings."

– MUHAMMAD ALI –

Dreams take time, patience,
sustained effort, and a willingness
to fail if they are ever to be
anything more than dreams.

EVERY DAY IS A
WONDERFUL CHANCE
TO BE WHAT
YOU'VE DREAMED...
TO DO WHAT
YOU'VE IMAGINED.

Don't rush yourself or your dream.
If you do everything today,
what will you do tomorrow?

To achieve all that is possible, you must attempt the *impossible*. To be all you can be, you must dream big. Don't let anyone scoff at your dream. Your dream is the promise of all you can become.

"Nothing splendid has ever been achieved except by those who dared believe that something inside them was superior to circumstance."

– BRUCE BARTON –

You bring something beautiful to the world,

something no one else can offer.

"Glory gives herself only to those who have always dreamed of her."

– CHARLES DE GAULLE –

"Endeavor to live so that when you die,
even the undertaker will be sorry."

– MARK TWAIN –

WHAT
WILL
YOUR
LEGACY
BE?

I hope my achievements in life shall be
these . . . that I fought for what was right
and fair, that I took risks for things
that mattered, that I helped those in need,
that I left the earth a better place
because of what I did and who I was.

★ DIS

COVER

Your future doesn't lie ahead of you,
waiting to happen. It lies deep inside of you,
waiting to be discovered.

"The best thing about the future is that
it comes only one day at a time."

– ABRAHAM LINCOLN –

LIFE IS
MORE INTERESTING
IF YOU DON'T
HAVE ALL
THE ANSWERS.

"Do not go where the path may lead;
go instead where there is no path
and leave a trail."

– RALPH WALDO EMERSON –

"Every calling is great when
greatly pursued."

– OLIVER WENDELL HOLMES –

"The important thing is to never stop questioning. Curiosity has its own reason for existing. One cannot help but be in awe when he contemplates the mysteries of eternity, of life, of the marvelous structure of reality. Never lose a holy curiosity."

– ALBERT EINSTEIN –

"Thinking is the hardest work there is — which is probably the reason so few engage in it."

– HENRY FORD –

Remember, while traveling the road to success,

it's fun to get a little lost along the way. In fact,

an explorer is someone who is always lost.

A really happy person is one who can enjoy
the scenery when on a detour.

"I merely took the energy it takes
to pout and wrote some blues."

– DUKE ELLINGTON –

"If a man does not keep pace with his
companions, perhaps it is because he
hears a different drummer. Let him
step to the music which he hears,
however measured or far away."

– HENRY DAVID THOREAU –

"Every now and then, go away; have a little relaxation. For when you come back to your work, your judgment will be surer, since to remain constantly at work, you lose power of judgment. Go some distance away, because then the work appears smaller, and more of it can be taken in at a glance, and a lack of harmony or proportion is more readily seen."

– LEONARDO DA VINCI –

NOBODY ELSE'S
FOOTSTEPS
LEAD EXACTLY
WHERE
YOU'RE GOING.

"One doesn't discover new lands without consenting to lose sight of the shore for a very long time."

– ANDRÉ GIDE –

"When you can do the common things
of life in an uncommon way, you will
command the attention of the world."

– GEORGE WASHINGTON CARVER –

★ DO

"Get out there and give real help! Get out there and love! Get out there and testify! Get out there and create whatever you can to inspire people to claim their divine being. This is what has to be done now. There is no time for dallying."

– MOTHER TERESA –

"One of life's great rules is this: The more you give, the more you get."

– WILLIAM H. DANFORTH –

"A life is not important except in the impact it has on other lives."

– JACKIE ROBINSON –

"We find in life exactly what
we put into it."

– RALPH WALDO EMERSON –

"Statistically, 100 percent of the shots
you don't take don't go in."

– WAYNE GRETZKY –

"Do not let what you cannot do
interfere with what you *can* do."

– COACH JOHN WOODEN –

Today you stand at a milestone in your life. Behind you are all the struggles and challenges you've conquered along the way. Before you lies a new horizon filled with thrilling possibilities. Today you choose the direction of your life. ***Go for it!***

"My life is my message."

– MAHATMA GANDHI –

"Always do right. This will gratify some people and astonish the rest."

– MARK TWAIN –

10 KEYS TO SUCCESS

1. BELIEVE WHEN OTHERS DOUBT.

2. LEARN WHILE OTHERS LOAF.

3. DECIDE WHILE OTHERS DELAY.

4. BEGIN WHILE OTHERS PROCRASTINATE.

5. WORK WHILE OTHERS WISH.

6. SAVE WHILE OTHERS SPEND.

7. LISTEN WHILE OTHERS TALK.

8. SMILE WHILE OTHERS SCOWL.

9. COMMEND WHILE OTHERS CRITICIZE.

10. PERSIST WHEN OTHERS QUIT.

Perhaps good things come to those who wait,

but the *best* things come to those who seize

the moment and make it their own.

Sometimes all that stands between you and
the ride of a lifetime is simply getting in the
saddle and seeing what you're made of.

A TO-DO LIST

SING.

SMILE AT STRANGERS.

KEEP LEARNING.

NOTICE KINDNESS.

EAT ICE CREAM.

HOPE.

COUNT YOUR BLESSINGS.

LAUGH.

LOVE.

LOVE SOME MORE.

To make a difference in this world,

you must first dare to be different.

When the truth needs to be spoken,

when the work needs to be done,

when the help needs to be offered . . .

dare to make a difference.

10 THINGS TO MAKE
BESIDES MONEY

1. TIME

2. MERRY

3. DO

4. UP

5. SENSE

6. PEACE

7. ROOM

8. WAVES

9. AMENDS

10. BELIEVE

Cherish your yesterdays, dream your tomorrows, but live your todays. Tomorrow belongs to those who fully use today.

Do what you love, and it will make your
soul rich.

Do what you'd do if you believed your every
dream could come true.
When you're doing
what you love, it feels like you're flying.

★ PERS

EVERE

"Success is never final. Failure is never fatal. It is courage that counts."

– WINSTON CHURCHILL –

"If you want the rainbow, you gotta put up with the rain."

– DOLLY PARTON –

"The only one who never makes
mistakes is the one who never
does anything."

– TEDDY ROOSEVELT –

"It's never too late to be what you
might have been."

– GEORGE ELIOT –

"It ain't over 'til it's over."

– YOGI BERRA –

"No one can make you feel inferior
without your consent."

– ELEANOR ROOSEVELT –

LIFE IS
A WORK IN
PROGRESS.

When you meet the small challenges of daily
living, you prepare yourself for the great
challenges of life.

"Progress comes from the intelligent
use of experience."

– ELBERT HUBBARD –

"I am a slow walker, but I never
walk backward."

– ABRAHAM LINCOLN –

"Don't look back. Something may
be gaining on you."

– SATCHEL PAIGE –

Look at life's challenges not as setbacks but

as opportunities to discover who you are.

"Life is a grindstone. But whether it grinds us down or polishes us up depends on us."

– THOMAS HOLDCRAFT –

"We must adjust to changing times but still hold to unchanging principles."

– JIMMY CARTER –

"A certain amount of opposition is a great help to a person. Kites rise against the wind, not with it."

– JOHN NEAL –

"Success isn't something you chase. It's something you have to put forth the effort for constantly. Then it'll come when you least expect it."

– MICHAEL JORDAN –

"Success is how high you bounce
when you hit bottom."

– GENERAL GEORGE S. PATTON –

"Success is often just an idea away."

– FRANK TYGER –

"I have learned that success is to be measured not so much by the position that one has reached in life as by the obstacles which he has overcome while trying to succeed."

– BOOKER T. WASHINGTON –

"Starting over is the bravest kind of starting there is."

– DAN TAYLOR –

"Courage is its own reward."

– PLAUTUS –

"With enough courage, you can do
without a reputation."

– CLARK GABLE –

"Never, never, never, never give up."

– WINSTON CHURCHILL –

"Obstacles cannot crush me.
Every obstacle yields to stern resolve.
He who is fixed to a star does not
change his mind."

– LEONARDO DA VINCI –

ENJOY

Let your success be measured by the
happiness in your heart.

"It is in the enjoyment and not in
the mere possession that makes
for happiness."

– MICHEL DE MONTAIGNE –

"I make myself rich by making
my wants few."

– HENRY DAVID THOREAU –

"The most wasted day is that on which one has not laughed."

– NICOLAS CHAMFORT –

"The happiness that comes from doing good is a happiness that will never end."

– CHINESE PROVERB –

"Laugh and grow strong."

– ST. IGNATIUS OF LOYOLA –

LOVE WHAT
YOU DO . . .

DO WHAT
YOU LOVE.

Remember . . . the world always looks brighter
from behind a smile.

"The world is like a mirror, you see?
Smile, and your friends smile back."

– ZEN PROVERB –

WE SMILE
BECAUSE WE
ARE HAPPY.
BUT WE ALSO
BECOME HAPPY
BECAUSE
WE SMILE.

Did you know?

A University of Maryland study showed that
while stress decreases blood flow in the
human body, experiencing humor increases
blood flow by 22 percent.

"Choose a job you love and you will never have to work a day in your life."

– CONFUCIUS –

A FINAL THOUGHT . . .

Don't forget to lift your eyes away from the keyboard
now and then to see how blue the sky is.

Don't forget to put away the cell and spend some time
with paintbrush, pen, or guitar.

Don't forget to seek the blessing of silence amid the rush
and noise of life.

And remember always that the secret of success is how
happily you climb — not how high.

If this book has inspired you, Hallmark would

love to hear about it. Write to us at 2501 McGee,

Mail Drop 215, Kansas City, MO 64141, or e-mail us at

booknotes@Hallmark.com. Tell us about your goals;

we'll hope along with you. Tell us about your

achievements; we'll celebrate with you.

Look for Hallmark Gift Books wherever

Hallmark products are sold.

ALBERTOSAURUS

by Kathryn Clay

CAPSTONE PRESS
a capstone imprint

Little Explorer is published by Capstone Press,
1710 Roe Crest Drive, North Mankato, Minnesota 56003
www.mycapstone.com

Library of Congress Cataloging-in-Publication Data
Library of Congress Cataloging-in-Publication data is available
on the Library of Congress website.
ISBN 978-1-5435-5747-3 (library binding)
ISBN 978-1-5435-6011-4 (paperback)
ISBN 978-1-5435-5754-1 (eBook PDF)

Editorial Credits
Michelle Parkin, editor; Lori Bye, designer;
Kelly Garvin, media researcher;
Kathy McColley, production specialist

Our very special thanks to Matthew T. Miller, Museum
Technician (Collections Volunteer Manager), Department
of Paleobiology at the National Museum of Natural History,
Smithsonian Institution, for his review. Capstone would also like
to thank Kealy Gordon, Product Development Manager, and the
following at Smithsonian Enterprises: Ellen Nanney, Licensing
Manager; Brigid Ferraro, Vice President, Education and Consumer
Products; and Carol LeBlanc, Senior Vice President, Education
and Consumer Products.

Image Credits
Alamy/Stephen J. Krasemann, 27; Getty Images: Bettmann, 28,
Richard Lautens/Contributor, 11; Jon Hughes, 1, 2, 5, 8, 10, 12-13,
13 (inset), 14-15, 16-17, 18, 19, 20, 23, 24, 30-31; Science Source: Arthur
Dorety/StocktrekImages, 14 (bottom), Millard H. Sharp, 25, Richard
T. Nowitz, 29; Shutterstock: Adwo, 5 (b), Herschel Hoffmeyer,
cover (background), leonello calvetti, 15, (top)(b), Linda Bucklin, 15,
(middle), Mariemily Photos, 26 (b), Warpaint, cover, 6-7; Wilkimedia/
Canadian Press Syndicate, 26 (t)

Printed and bound in the USA.
PA48

TABLE OF CONTENTS

DINO FILE

name: Albertosaurus

how to say it: al-BER-tuh-SAWR-us

when it lived: Late Cretaceous Period, Mesozoic Era

what it ate: meat

size: up to 33 feet (10 meters) long

weighed 2 to 3 tons

up to 12 feet (3.5 m) tall

Albertosaurus was a dangerous predator. It was half the size of Tyrannosaurus rex but just as deadly.

Thanks to FOSSILS

A fossil is evidence of life from the past. Fossil bones, teeth, and tracks found in the earth have taught us everything we know about dinosaurs.

Albertosaurus skull

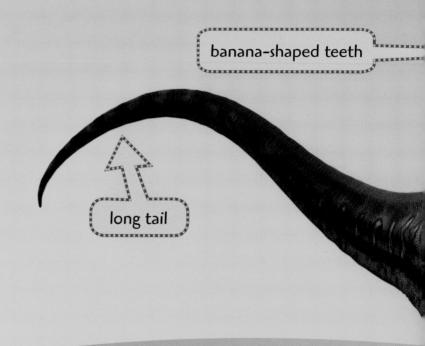

banana-shaped teeth

long tail

powerful back legs

STANDING TALL

Albertosaurus belonged to a group
of dinosaurs called theropods.
Other dinosaurs in this group include
Tyrannosaurus rex and Allosaurus.

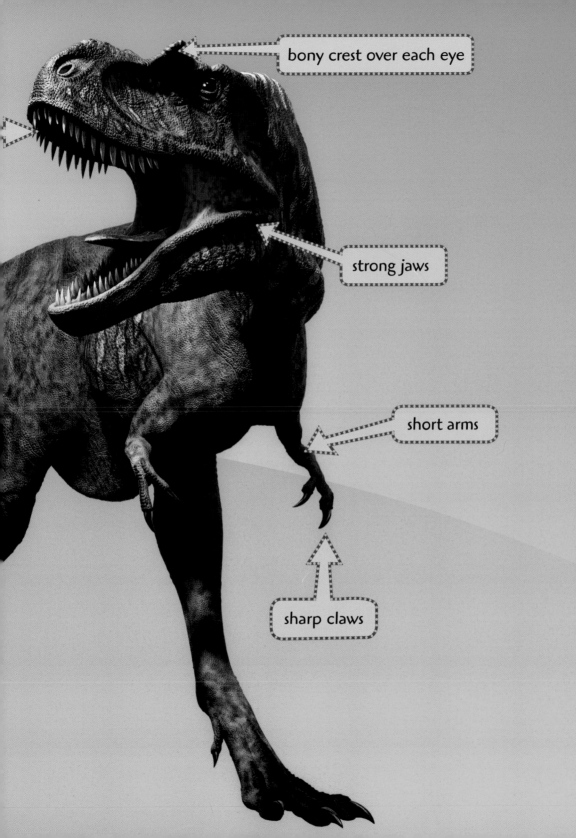

bony crest over each eye

strong jaws

short arms

sharp claws

ONE HUGE HEAD

Albertosaurus had a large
head compared to its body.
Its skull was 3.3 feet (1 m) long.
The dinosaur's short neck
was shaped like the letter S.
Albertosaurus's brain was larger
than those of earlier dinosaurs.

Albertosaurus had a short, bony
crest over each eye. Scientists think
the crest was brightly colored.
Albertosaurus may have used its
crest to attract a mate.

CHOMP!

Albertosaurus had strong, powerful jaws. They held up to 60 banana-shaped teeth. Albertosaurus's teeth had serrated edges that ripped into prey.

Scientists believe the dinosaur also bit into other Albertosauruses. They discovered Albertosaurus jaw bones with deep scars. The marks were caused by another Albertosaurus.

When Albertosaurus lost a tooth, a new one grew in its place.

an Albertosaurus tooth next to six raptor teeth

TINY HANDS

Like other theropods, Albertosaurus's arms were much shorter than its legs. At the end of each tiny hand, the dinosaur had two clawed fingers.

Some scientists think Albertosaurus used its arms to hold down prey. Others think the dinosaur used its arms to get off the ground after sleeping.

Theropods are often shown with their hands facing down in drawings and movies. This is not correct. Scientists believe a theropod held its hands sideways with its palms facing each other.

13

A HUMID HOME

Albertosaurus lived during the Late Cretaceous Period. Large and small dinosaurs roamed the Earth during this time. Insects, mammals, and birds first appeared. The weather was hot and wet. Huge tropical plants covered the ground.

Albertosaurus made its home in the western part of North America in what is now Alberta, Canada.

The name Albertosaurus means *Alberta lizard.*

OTHER CRETACEOUS DINOSAURS

Ankylosaurus

Triceratops

Velociraptor

The Cretaceous Period lasted from 145 million to 66 million years ago.

DINOSAUR ERA

TRIASSIC	JURASSIC	CRETACEOUS

252   200   145   66   present

millions of years ago

TOP OF THE FOOD CHAIN

Albertosaurus was a carnivore. This means it ate only meat. As the largest dinosaur in the area, Albertosaurus was considered an apex predator. This means it had no predators. Rather than worry about safety, it spent most of its time hunting.

Albertosaurus preferred to catch its dinner. But this dinosaur was also a scavenger. If live prey wasn't available, Albertosaurus ate animals that were already dead.

Albertosaurus ate dinosaurs such as Pachyrhinosaurus, Edmontosaurus, and Lambeosaurus.

T. REX RELATIVE

Tyrannosaurus rex was closely related to Albertosaurus. But the two did not live during the same time. Albertosaurus lived about 8 million years before T. rex.

Tyrannosaurus rex

The two dinosaurs looked similar, but there were a number of differences:

- Albertosaurus had a more slender, smaller head and body.

- Albertosaurus ran much faster than T. rex.

- Albertosaurus had a large crest above each eye.

- Albertosaurus had more teeth than T. rex.

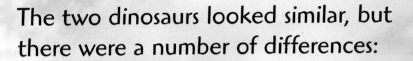

Albertosaurus

SPEEDY PREDATOR

Albertosaurus moved quickly on its two back legs. It could run up to 25 miles (40 kilometers) per hour.

The dinosaur chased down fast prey. Albertosaurus could use the sharp claws on its back legs to deliver deadly strikes.

PACK ATTACK

Scientists believe Albertosaurus could have lived in packs. Large groups of Albertosaurus fossils have been found together.

Living in packs helped make hunting easier. It's possible that faster, younger Albertosaurus chased prey toward the slower, stronger adults. Then the adults would attack the prey.

Albertosaurus had a growth spurt from the age of 12 to 16.

ALBERTOSAURUS LIFE CYCLE

Little is known about young Albertosaurus. Few baby and juvenile fossils have been found. One reason could be because their bones were not as solid as adult bones. They broke apart and were not well preserved.

It's also possible that most Albertosauruses grew into adults. Without any predators, they were able to live long lives. The oldest Albertosaurus found was about 28 years old when it died.

The youngest Albertosaurus fossil ever found was from a two-year-old dinosaur. So far no Albertosaurus eggs have been discovered.

theropod eggs

DINO DISCOVERY

The first Albertosaurus fossil was discovered in 1884. Geologist J.B. Tyrrell found part of an Albertosaurus skull in the Horseshoe Canyon Formation in Alberta, Canada. This was the first meat-eating dinosaur fossil found in Canada.

J.B. Tyrrell

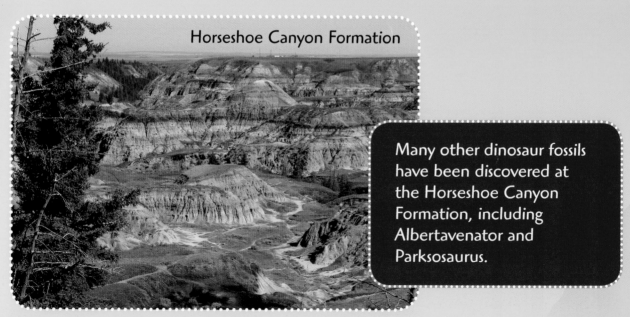

Horseshoe Canyon Formation

Many other dinosaur fossils have been discovered at the Horseshoe Canyon Formation, including Albertavenator and Parksosaurus.

In 1889 Thomas Chesmer Weston found
another Albertosaurus skull in Alberta.
These skulls were originally labeled as
another dinosaur, Laelaps. Paleontologist
Henry Osborn renamed the fossils
"Albertosaurus" in 1905.

A SECOND LOOK

In 1910 paleontologist Barnum Brown discovered a bone bed in Alberta. He dug up bones from nine different Albertosaurus skeletons. But over time, the bone bed's location was lost and forgotten.

Barnum Brown discovered the first Tyrannosaurus rex fossil in 1902. He found so many dinosaur bones during his career that he was giving the nickname "Mr. Bones."

Scientists Philip Currie and Eva Koppelhus dig for Albertosaurus bones in Alberta.

Nearly 90 years later paleontologist Philip Currie used photographs from Brown's dig to find the bone bed. Currie and his team discovered more than 1,500 fossils in what is now called the Dry Island bone bed. Most of the fossils were from Albertosaurus. A few hadrosaur fossils were also found.

"It really is exciting to see something nobody's seen before, like finding buried treasure."

—paleontologist Philip Currie

GLOSSARY

apex predator (AY-peks PRED-uh-tur)—an animal that is not preyed on by any other animal

bone bed (BOHN BED)—a single layer of rock that contains a large number of fossils

carnivore (KAHR-nuh-vohr)—an animal that eats only meat

crest (KREST)—a comb or tuft of feathers, bone, or skin on the head of a bird or other animal

fossil (FAH-suhl)—evidence of life from the geologic past

geologist (jee-AHL-uh-jist)—a scientist who studies minerals, rocks, and soil

juvenile (JOO-vuh-nuhl)—describing a young person or animal

mate (MATE)—one of a pair of animals that have young

Mesozoic Era (mehz-uh-ZOH-ik IHR-uh)—the age of dinosaurs which includes the Triassic, Jurassic, and Cretaceous periods; when the first birds, mammals, and flowers appeared

paleontologist (pale-ee-uhn-TOL-uh-jist)—a scientist who studies fossils

pack (PAK)—a group of animals that hunts together

palm (PALM)—the flat, inside part of a hand

predator (PRED-uh-tur)—an animal that hunts other animals for food

prey (PRAY)—an animal that is hunted by another animal for food

relative (REL-uh-tiv)—belonging to the same family or group

scavenger (SKAV-uhn-jer)—an animal that feeds on animals that are already dead

theropod (THAIR-oh-pod)—a member of a group of dinosaurs that walked or ran on two legs; most theropods ate meat

tropical (TRAH-pi-kuhl)—hot, wet, and humid

CRITICAL THINKING QUESTIONS

1. Albertosaurus looked similar to Tyrannosaurus rex. Compare Albertosaurus to another theropod, Allosaurus. How are the dinosaurs similar? How are they different?

2. Paleontologist Henry Osborn gave Albertosaurus its name in 1905. List two other dinosaurs Osborn named.

3. In addition to Albertosaurus bones, Philip Currie found hadrosaur fossils at the Dry Island bone bed. What are hadrosaurs?

READ MORE

Johnson, Jinny. *Mighty Killers.* Discovering Dinosaurs. Mankato, MN: Smart Apple Media, 2014.

Peterson, Megan Cooley. *Tyrannosaurus Rex and Its Relatives: The Need-to-Know Facts.* Dinosaur Fact Dig. North Mankato, MN: Capstone Press, 2016.

Switek, Brian. *The T. Rex Handbook.* Kennebunkport, ME: Applesauce Press, 2016.

INTERNET SITES

Use FactHound to find Internet sites related to this book.

Visit *www.facthound.com*

Just type in 9781543557473 and go.

Check out projects, games and lots more at
www.CAPSTONEKIDS.com

INDEX